Happy Cooking
Evelyn

The Magic of Spices

Healthful, Delicious Vegetarian Meals in the Indian-American Style

by
Evelyn Banker

Next title appearing soon

Copyright © 2008 Evelyn Banker

ISBN: 978-0-615-28356-2

All rights reserved.
No part of this book may be reproduced
in any form, by photostat, microfilm,
xerography, or any other means,
or incorporated into any information retrieval
system, electronic or mechanical, without the
written permission of the copyright owner.

All inquiries should be addressed to :
Evelyn Banker
86-27 55th Road,
Elmhurst, New York,
11373 USA

Published by
Evelyn Banker

Printing managed by
Star Print Brokers, Inc.
www.StarPrintBrokers.com

Printed in
Republic of Korea

CREDITS

Photography
Food Preparation
Props and Styling by the Author
Evelyn Banker

Concept, cover and book design
Dollly Biswas

Editor
Steven Mason

Evelyn Banker

Expert Cooking Teacher
Specializing in
Medicinal Value of Spices

Email : evelynbanker@magicofspices.com
Evelyn's website is www.magicofspices.com

Acknowledgements

My Daddy, who has always been a pillar of strength.

My husband Steven, who showed me how to put my ideas into words.

My children, Mallika and Akshay, who found beauty in my simple ways.

My sisters and brothers, Grace, Joan, Alice, Sunny, Eddie, Dorothy, Valentina and Loretta, who helped me grow.

My friend Dolly, who believed in me and helped me believe in myself.

My friend Kailash, who helped turn my words into a book.

My first American friend, Haydee, who helped me to see the value of my knowledge.

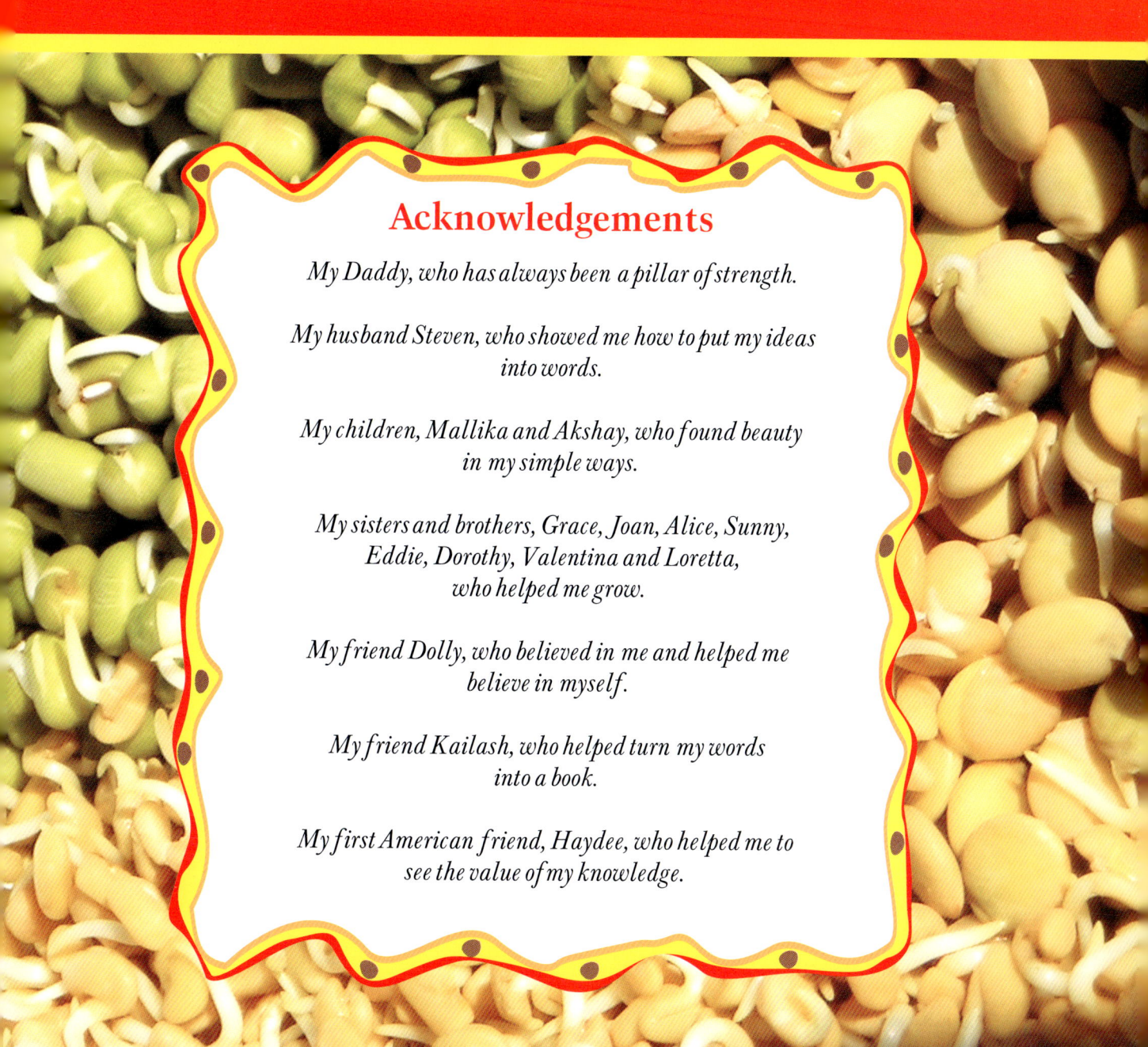

Introduction

Welcome to my cookbook!

Every recipe in this book contains ingredients that have important medicinal value, but don't let that scare you away – they are also delicious. You'll see.

First, I want to make it clear that I am not a scientist or a nutritionist, and that there is nothing new in what I will be telling you about the medicinal value of my recipes. On the contrary, these things have been known for thousands of years. In the last few decades, however, much of this knowledge has been forgotten, and it is only gradually being rediscovered.

One good example of what I mean is turmeric.

In India, where I was born, it has been used for centuries as a versatile medication, an antiseptic and anti-inflammatory agent. Turmeric can aid in the healing of broken bones, and can be used to stop bleeding. Studies have shown that turmeric can reduce the incidence of Alzheimer's disease and other similar conditions. It also figures prominently in many spiritual and religious rituals. In addition to its wonderful flavor and medicinal value, turmeric also adds a beautiful touch of color to any dish. Just a pinch of turmeric in your diet every day will make a world of difference.

The simple, yet delicious and healthful style of cooking that I present in this book was taught to me by my mother. I am one of nine children, and we lived on a small farm in an isolated area in the little town of Kota, in the state of Rajasthan, India. We had no access to store-bought food, and lived almost exclusively on what we grew. The grains, dals and legumes you will be using in these recipes were our everyday diet (plus chicken once a week). I saw my mother use simple, natural methods of healing (such as a preparation of turmeric to treat the injured leg of a goat). We prepared our food so that it could be used all year round -- in summer, we had homemade potato chips and snacks made from dal batter that was dried in the sun. In the monsoon season, there would be plenty of grains, and pickle (relish) made from mango, papaya, guava and other fruits. The wheat and rice we bought lasted for a full year, and nourished the chickens as well as the family.

When I became a mother, I fed my own children much the same diet. They never ate processed foods, only home-cooked meals made fresh every day. This diet maintained their good health, and kept them from becoming overweight. Also, many of my friends and students have been able to get rid of various conditions that had long bothered them, such as rashes and other recurring skin problems, simply by eating and enjoying these dishes. The spices you will be using are not overpowering, simply flavorful and aromatic. They will improve your digestion, and that will enhance your overall well-being.

Remember, "spice" does not mean "spicy".

In the span of my life, I have known and made use of both ancient and modern cooking methods. Because of this, I am able to appreciate how much simpler, faster and more convenient it is to prepare these dishes today than it was years ago. The availability of ground spices, which we didn't have when I was a child, as well as the use of the pressure cooker and other time-saving kitchen tools, means that any dish in this book can be prepared in a fraction of the time it would have taken way back then. And once you have become familiar with the ingredients used in these recipes, you will be able to create your own variations.

And now, on to the recipes!*

**All recipes in this book are for two servings.*

Table of Contents

Chapter One	–	Chutneys	Page 1
Chapter Two	–	Soups	Page 10
Chapter Three	–	Grains	Page 21
Chapter Four	–	Crêpes	Page 29
Chapter Five	–	Side Dishes	Page 32
Chapter Six	–	Squash	Page 42
Chapter Seven	–	Beans	Page 45
Chapter Eight	–	Sauces	Page 48
Chapter Nine	–	Fries	Page 52
Chapter Ten	–	Roti	Page 56
Chapter Eleven	–	Chai	Page 58
Chapter Twelve	–	Tips	Page 62
Chapter Thirteen	–	Medicinal Values	Page 64
Chapter Fourteen	–	A Final Word	Page 67

Indian Spices and Ingredients

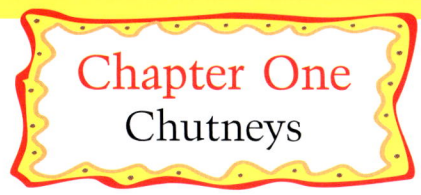
Chapter One
Chutneys

Here are a few of the many chutneys *(also called dips, spreads, relishes, or whichever word you prefer)* that are used in Indian cuisine to open your taste buds and pep up any meal. Since my mother always started the day by grinding her turmeric, I will start my book with a delicious relish made from this "King of Spices".

Fresh Turmeric

Turmeric Relish

3 or 4 two-inch pieces of fresh turmeric
Juice of ½ lemon
Salt to taste
One ½ inch piece of ginger (optional)

Grate the turmeric (and ginger, if desired) or slice it into thin pieces. Put it into a bowl, add lemon juice and salt, mix well. If you won't be using it all at once, keep the remainder in the fridge.

Remember that ginger is quite strong and spicy, especially raw ginger, but I love the combination of turmeric and ginger.

In addition to turmeric relish, you can also make turmeric juice by putting a few pieces of fresh turmeric in a juicer; you can drink this plain or mix it with other juices. Also, you can add fresh shredded turmeric to any salad.

Yogurt with Cumin

1 cup plain yogurt
½ tsp. cumin seeds
Salt and pepper to taste

Toast the cumin seeds in a skillet over a low flame for about half a minute. Remove from heat, grind the seeds in a coffee grinder. Sprinkle seeds over the yogurt. Add any vegetables you like, or enjoy it plain.

Yogurt and Mint

1 cup plain yogurt
Handful of mint
2 or 3 cloves of garlic
Salt and pepper to taste

Grind the garlic and mint leaves together; mix well into yogurt. Salt and pepper to taste.

(You can also add cucumber, tomato, carrot, onion, etc. to turn a dip into a salad, or add diced boiled potato to make potato salad.)

Cilantro/Mint Spread

Large bunch of cilantro
Large bunch of mint
1 tsp. dry-ground cumin seeds
4 cloves of garlic (or more, to taste)
Juice of 1½ lemons or limes
(or more, to taste)
Salt and pepper to taste
Pinch of sugar

Combine all ingredients, grind together to a spread consistency. Serve as is, or mix with yogurt. Add shredded coconut or ground peanuts and/or pine nuts, if desired. This can be used to make sandwiches; just spread on bread, add cucumber, tomato, boiled potato and cheese, if desired. Delicious.

Carrot Relish

½ lb. carrots
1 tsp. crushed mustard seeds
Pinch of turmeric
Pinch of salt
3 to 4 cups water

Wash carrots, then cut into slivers, or any shape you choose. In a mixing bowl, combine carrots, mustard seeds, turmeric and salt. Put into a large jar. Boil water, then cool water down to room temperature. Add water to carrot mixture, let it stand for a day or two. (*In warm weather, less time is needed for fermentation.*)
The relish will keep indefinitely.

Cabbage Relish

½ *cabbage head (finely chopped)*
1 tsp. mustard seeds (cleaned and split)
4 or 5 tsps. mustard oil
Salt and pepper to taste

Combine cabbage, mustard seeds, salt and pepper in a large mixing bowl. Put into a large bottle or jar; add mustard oil till mixture is covered. Let stand for a day or two. It will taste as good as it looks (*and it will look great*)!

Cranberry Chutney

1 cup fresh cranberries
¼ inch piece of ginger, finely sliced
½ tsp. powdered cinnamon
¼ tsp. powdered clove
Pinch of powdered nutmeg
Sugar or honey to taste
Water
Pinch of salt

In a saucepan, combine cranberries with just enough water to cover them, cook over high flame till it boils, then lower heat and add cinnamon, clove, nutmeg and salt. Continue cooking till desired thickness is achieved. Serve hot, cold or at room temperature.

Date Chutney

½ cup seedless dates (soaked in water for about 2 hrs.)
½ tsp. tamarind paste
2 or 3 cloves
¼ tsp. coriander seeds
Sugar to taste
Pinch of salt
Water

Put all ingredients into a food processor, grind to desired thickness.

Seedless Dates

Mango Chutney

1 large mango, diced or grated
⅛ tsp. mustard seeds
⅛ tsp. cumin seeds
⅛ tsp. fenugreek seeds
⅛ tsp. fennel seeds
⅛ tsp. kalonji (schwartzkornel) seeds
Crushed pepper to taste
Salt to taste
Pinch of turmeric
Pinch of sugar
Pinch of asafoetida (heeng)
1 tbsp. cooking oil

Heat oil in saucepan. Add all seeds. When seeds pop, add crushed pepper, asafoetida, turmeric, mango, sugar and salt. Cook over medium flame for 2 to 3 minutes. Serve hot or at room temperature.

Mango, carrot or cabbage chutney can also be added to any grain salad (see Chapter 3). It will make it even more delicious!
If you like, you can add a handful of dried cranberries along with the mango. It will take the chutney to another level.

Flax Seeds

When I was little, my mother would feed flax seed cakes to the goats to improve the quality of their milk. She would also grind flax seeds and mix them with wheat to make flour for bread. Now that the value of flax seeds is generally known, here are a few suggestions on how to use them. (*First, grind the flax seeds in a coffee grinder.*)

Smoothie with Flax Seeds

½ cup plain yogurt
1 banana
6-8 strawberries (or any berries you like)
2 tsps. ground flax seeds
Honey to taste
Water, if needed

Put all ingredients into blender, blend to desired consistency. You can vary this by using orange juice or milk instead of yogurt, and you can create your own recipe by using almost any kind of fruit you choose.

Ground flax seeds can also be added to hot or cold cereal or yogurt, or stirred into a glass of milk. They are also great mixed in with plain fruit juice.

Tukmaria Seeds

These are a form of basil seed. They should be soaked in water for ten minutes or so (*if you soak them longer than that, it's OK*); they will become gelatinous and can be mixed into yogurt, cereal, smoothie or salad. No cooking is required; soaking the seeds makes them nice and soft. In hot weather, they have a wonderful cooling effect -- you can just drink them down in a glass of cold water. If you want to be a little naughty, mix tukmaria seeds into some ice cream!

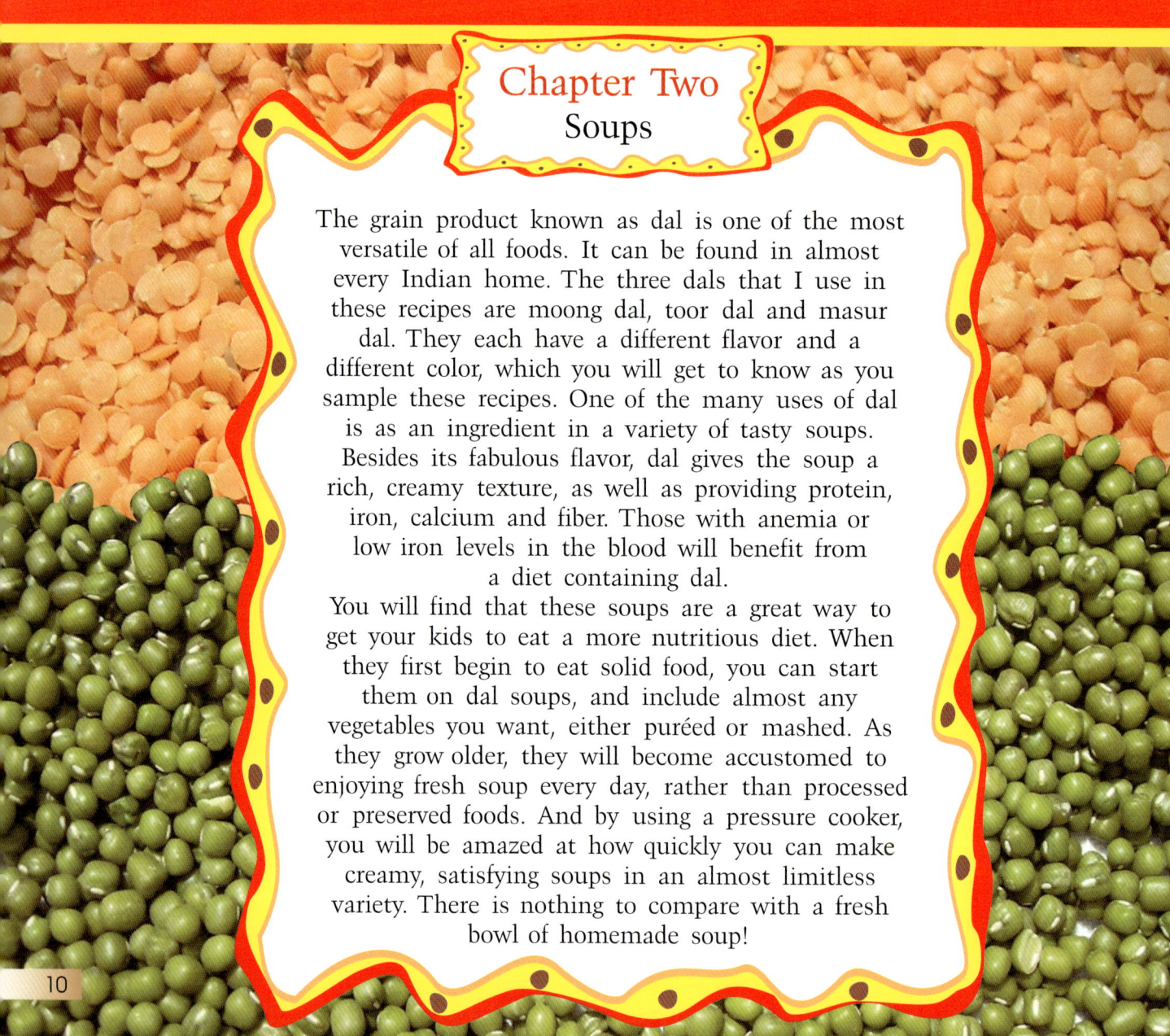

Chapter Two
Soups

The grain product known as dal is one of the most versatile of all foods. It can be found in almost every Indian home. The three dals that I use in these recipes are moong dal, toor dal and masur dal. They each have a different flavor and a different color, which you will get to know as you sample these recipes. One of the many uses of dal is as an ingredient in a variety of tasty soups. Besides its fabulous flavor, dal gives the soup a rich, creamy texture, as well as providing protein, iron, calcium and fiber. Those with anemia or low iron levels in the blood will benefit from a diet containing dal.

You will find that these soups are a great way to get your kids to eat a more nutritious diet. When they first begin to eat solid food, you can start them on dal soups, and include almost any vegetables you want, either puréed or mashed. As they grow older, they will become accustomed to enjoying fresh soup every day, rather than processed or preserved foods. And by using a pressure cooker, you will be amazed at how quickly you can make creamy, satisfying soups in an almost limitless variety. There is nothing to compare with a fresh bowl of homemade soup!

All dals come in three forms - whole, split, split and cleaned -
and you can do wonderful things with them.
Each dal has its own color, its own texture and its own flavor.

Toor Dal (Pigeon Pea) Soup

1 cup toor dal
4 cups water
½ inch piece of ginger, grated
½ tsp. turmeric powder
Pinch of asafoetida (heeng)
Salt and pepper to taste
Cilantro

Put dal and water into saucepan. Add ginger and turmeric (if you prefer, you can put in a whole piece of ginger, then remove it when soup is cooked). Cook over high flame till it comes to a boil, about 10 minutes, then simmer for 15 to 20 minutes. Remove from flame. Add cilantro. Serve hot.

For a garnish, heat 1 tsp. oil in a saucepan; add ⅛ tsp. each of mustard seeds, cumin seeds and curry leaves, plus 1 clove of garlic, finely chopped, and a pinch of asafoetida. Heat for about a minute over a low flame, till seeds pop and mixture becomes nice and brown. Add to soup.

Toor Dal (Pigeon Pea) Soup

Creamy Toor Dal Soup with Onions and Tomatoes

1 cup toor dal
4 cups water
Pinch of turmeric
1 small onion or shallot, finely chopped
1 large tomato, finely chopped
1 small carrot, shredded
¼ cup peas (optional)
¼ tsp. cumin seeds
Salt and pepper to taste
Lemon juice to taste
1 tbsp. oil (preferably olive oil, but any cooking oil will do)

Put dal, water and turmeric into saucepan. Heat over high flame till boiling, then lower flame and cook for about 20 minutes. When dal is creamy, remove from fire, add more water till desired consistency is reached. Heat oil in a frying pan, add cumin seeds. When seeds pop, lower flame and add onion or shallot, cook till translucent. Combine with dal mixture. Add tomatoes and peas (if desired), cook about 5 minutes. Remove from heat, add carrot, mix well. Add salt and pepper and lemon juice in desired amounts.

Toor Dal Soup with Pesto

1 cup toor dal
4 cups water
Pinch of turmeric
Handful of basil leaves
3 or 4 cloves of garlic
(or more if desired)
Salt and pepper to taste
Lemon juice to taste
2 tbsps. olive oil (or more if desired)

Put dal, water and turmeric into saucepan. Heat over high flame till boiling, then lower flame and cook for about 20 minutes. To make pesto, place basil leaves, garlic, salt, pepper and lemon juice into food processor. Process till mixed well, add olive oil. Place in bowl. Serve alongside the soup, and add pesto to soup in desired amounts.

If the dal is cooked in a pressure cooker, it will take about half as long to prepare, and the texture will be even creamier. Plus, you will be using less energy. Just follow the manufacturer's directions. And if the toor dal is soaked for about 15 minutes beforehand, the cooking time is reduced by about half.

You will find that these dal soups can be enjoyed by anyone of any age from infancy onward. Once you have learned these simple soups, you can create different variations by adding lemon juice or your favorite vegetables and greens (carrots, peas, celery, or any leafy greens).
Invent your own versions!

Whole Green Moong Dal Soup

1 cup moong dal
4 cups water
½ tsp. turmeric powder
2 or 3 cloves of garlic
Salt and pepper to taste

Put dal into saucepan, add water, turmeric powder and garlic. Cook over high flame till it comes to a boil, about 10 minutes, then over low flame till dal is tender, about 20 to 30 minutes. Remove from flame, add more water if desired. Serve hot.

Split, Skinless and Whole Green Moong Dal

Whole Green Moong Dal Soup

Masur Dal (Split Skinless Lentils) Soup

1 cup masur dal
4 cups water
½ tsp. turmeric powder
1 large onion, chopped
Salt and pepper to taste
½ tsp. cumin seeds
(toasted and crushed)

Put dal and water into saucepan, add turmeric powder and onion. Cook over high flame for about 10 minutes, then over low flame for about 15 to 20 minutes. Remove from heat. Add salt and pepper, garnish with cumin seeds.

Masur Dal (Split Skinless Lentils) Soup

Split (Skinless) Moong Dal Soup with Quinoa*

¼ cup moong dal
4 cups water
¼ cup quinoa
3 carrots, diced
¼ cup peas, frozen or fresh
1 celery stalk, diced
1 large potato, diced
5 bok choy flowers
½ tsp. turmeric powder
Pinch of nutmeg
½ tsp. cumin seeds
Salt and pepper to taste
1 tsp. olive oil

*Quinoa is a cereal grain from Peru. It is high in protein and low in fat. It can be found in many large food markets.

Put dal, turmeric powder, cumin seeds and nutmeg into water, cook in saucepan over high flame till it boils, then lower flame and cook for 5 to 10 minutes till dal softens. Add carrots, celery and potato, cook till fork-tender, about 10 minutes. Add quinoa, cook for 5 more minutes. Add peas, cook 1 more minute, then add bok choy, cook 2 to 5 minutes, remove from heat, add salt and pepper. Put into bowls, drizzle with olive oil.

Chapter Three
Grains

The different varieties of grains that are used in these recipes have several things in common. They are all easy to store, quick and simple to cook, and very versatile (they can be mixed with a great many other ingredients). For example, green moong dal can be used in soups, salads, or as a side dish in a pilaf. And cracked wheat, millet, finger millet (raghi) and quinoa can be used in both sweet dishes (porridge) and savory dishes (pilaf).

While all grains are easy to use, both beans and chick peas must be washed and soaked overnight, and require more cooking time than dal.

The recipes I am presenting are some of my favorites, and they will introduce you to a few of the ways in which grains have been used in Indian cuisine for centuries. But remember, that is only the beginning. Once you become familiar with these grains, you can vary and combine them to create dishes that will perfectly suit your own tastes.

Sprouts

Any whole grain can be used to make sprouts. Simply wash the grain and soak it overnight in a large amount of water. Next morning, drain it and put it in a warm, dark place *(I keep mine in the oven)*. By the next day, you will see the baby sprouts coming up! These can be used in salads just as they are, or cooked as a side dish, as follows:

2 cups of moong dal sprouts (also known as mung beans)
1 small onion, sliced
2 cloves of garlic, crushed or sliced
¼ tsp. turmeric powder
Handful of button mushrooms, sliced (optional)
Handful of cherry or grape tomatoes
2 tbsps. cooking oil (any kind)
Salt and pepper to taste

Put oil in a skillet on medium heat, then add onions. As the onions become translucent, add garlic and mushrooms, lower flame. After a minute or so, when mushrooms are nice and brown, add turmeric and sprouts, then salt and pepper; stir well. Remove from heat right away for crunchy sprouts, or leave on low heat till tender enough to suit your taste. Add tomatoes as soon as you turn off the heat. Can be enjoyed hot or at room temperature.

The rich and varied world of sprouts

Wheat Salad

1 cup cracked wheat
2 cups water
1 tbsp. olive oil
1 lemon
¼ cup fresh pomegranate seeds
1 large carrot, shredded
Salt and pepper to taste

Toast cracked wheat over low heat in skillet till brown (about 10 minutes); raise heat and add 2 cups of water. When it boils, lower flame, stir, cover pan and cook till water is dissolved (about 20 minutes). Stir with fork; let cool. Mix in all other ingredients (put in any additions you like, such as raisins, cranberries, nuts). Great at any temperature.

Hot Cracked Wheat

1 cup cracked wheat
2 cups water
1 small onion, finely chopped
1 cup peas and chopped carrots, mixed
Pinch of turmeric powder
¼ tsp. mustard seeds
2 tbsps. oil
Salt and pepper to taste

Heat the wheat in a skillet till brown (about 10 minutes). Remove from skillet into a dish. Heat oil in skillet, add mustard seeds; when seeds pop, add onions; when they are translucent, add turmeric powder, then peas and carrots, water and wheat. When it boils, lower flame, cover pan and cook for 20 minutes. Add salt and pepper to taste.

This can be varied by using millet, rice or any other grains instead of wheat, and by adding your favorite dals and vegetables.

Corn Meal Salad

1 cup corn meal or cream of wheat (farina)
⅓ cup peas
⅓ cup dried cranberries
¼ tsp. mustard seeds
1 small onion, finely chopped
6 to 8 cherry tomatoes
Pinch of turmeric
2 tsps. cooking oil
2 cups water
Lemon juice, olive oil and salt to taste

Toast corn meal in dry skillet over low flame for 8 to 10 minutes. Remove from heat. In another skillet, put in oil, heat for about ½ minute over high flame, add mustard seeds. Lower flame and add onion. When onion becomes translucent (about a minute), add corn meal and turmeric, stir for a minute, then add water, raise flame, add peas and cranberries, stir for about 3 to 5 minutes till water is absorbed. Remove from heat. Fluff with fork, add cherry tomatoes, drizzle with olive oil, add lemon juice and salt if desired.

Grain Porridge

½ cup cracked wheat
¼ cup millet
¼ cup quinoa
1 stick of cinnamon
2 cups water

In a sturdy saucepan, toast all the grains over a low flame for about 5 minutes. Add water, raise flame, bring to boil. Add cinnamon stick, stir well. Lower flame, cover pan and cook for 20 minutes. For a sweet dish, after cooking, add milk, sugar or honey (or berries and fruit); for a savory dish, add olive oil and your favorite vegetables or dried berries with salt and pepper, or serve as is.

Sprouts Salad

1 cup moong dal sprouts
½ cup fenugreek seed sprouts
1 red onion, finely chopped
1 large tomato, cut into bite-size pieces
Seeds of 1 fresh pomegranate (optional)
Juice of 1½ lemons or limes
Mint, coriander or parsley (if desired), for garnish
Salt and pepper to taste
2 to 3 tsps. olive oil or flaxseed oil

The ingredients in this salad are so fresh and full of juices that you may not even need the oil.

Mix all ingredients together thoroughly in a large bowl and enjoy!

Chapter Four
Crêpes

Here are five different kinds of dal which can be used to make crêpes: masoor, toor, urad, channa and moong. They can be purchased already cleaned, skinned and split; then they must be soaked for at least 2 hours. Or you can use any kind of flour (whole wheat, raghi, chick pea, etc.).
If you use flour, add a little oil to the batter if needed (the crêpe will tell you if it needs any oil).
Here is one of my favorite crêpe recipes.

Five-Dal Crêpes

All 5 types of dal (¼ cup each)
Water
Cooking oil
Salt and pepper (if desired)

After dals have been soaked for a minimum of 2 hours, grind them in a food processor or blender with enough water to create the consistency of a dip. Add salt and pepper if you prefer, but the crêpes will be very flavorful without any seasoning. Heat a pan or griddle. Use a paper towel to coat the surface of the pan with oil. Put 2 tablespoons of the batter onto the griddle for each crêpe. Use the back of a large spoon to spread the batter into a crêpe. Cook over a medium flame for about 1½ minutes on each side, depending on how soft or how crisp you like your crêpes. Before turning the crêpe, put a few drops of oil around it. When done, immediately remove from heat.

Here are some other variations of the crêpe batter:

⅓ cup of urad dal, soaked and ground, plus ⅔ cup of wheat farina. Mix with spoon till smooth.

1 cup of farina mixed with 1 cup of yogurt; add water if needed for smoothness. If desired, you can add chopped onions, tomato or cilantro. Salt and pepper to taste.

1 cup urad dal plus 2 cups plain uncooked rice. Soak and grind separately (the rice will need a little more soaking than the dal), then mix together. Add salt if needed.

In the chick pea batter, you can add finely chopped onion and tomato, and a pinch of carom seeds, plus salt and pepper to taste.

These crêpes can be filled with a great variety of ingredients.
Some suggestions:
Cottage cheese mixed with honey
Cream cheese and jelly or preserves
Leftover vegetables
Pesto
Or create your own fillings

Any leftover batter can be kept in the fridge for a couple of days, so you can have hot crêpes whenever you like. They are good for any meal, or as a snack.
Children will love them.

Chapter Five
Side Dishes

These side dishes make use of some familiar ingredients, but in different ways than you may be accustomed to. Try them in place of your usual side dishes and enjoy the difference!

Turmeric Salad

2 to 3 inch piece of fresh turmeric, cleaned, peeled and shredded
2 celery stalks, finely chopped
½ cup each of moong dal sprouts and fenugreek sprouts
¼ head of lettuce, chopped
1 small cucumber, diced
1 cup cherry tomatoes

Mix all ingredients together in a large bowl; add olive oil and lemon, or whatever dressing you like. You can vary the ingredients any way you want, but don't forget the turmeric!

Okra with Mustard Seeds

1 lb. okra
½ tsp. mustard seeds
¼ tsp. turmeric powder
1 tbsp. cooking oil (any kind)
Salt and pepper to taste
Curry leaves (optional)
Lemon juice to taste

Wash okra, dry thoroughly with a paper towel, then dice. Heat oil in frying pan, add mustard seeds and curry leaves (if desired), turmeric powder, and okra. Stir-fry over medium heat till okra is tender, about 10 minutes. Add lemon juice, salt and pepper to taste.

Okra with Mustard Seeds

Green Beans and Potatoes

¼ lb. green beans
2 medium-sized potatoes
1 large tomato, diced
8 to 10 cherry tomatoes
1 tbsp. cooking oil (any kind)
1 small onion
2 or 3 cloves of garlic
½ inch piece of ginger
¼ tsp. turmeric powder

Peel and dice potatoes. Remove string from green beans, cut beans into small pieces, finely chop onion. Peel the garlic and ginger and make a paste by grinding in blender *(see Chapter 12)*. Heat oil in pan, fry onions, add garlic and ginger paste, turmeric powder, then potatoes, beans and diced tomato. Cook over medium heat till tender, about 15 to 20 minutes. Add salt and pepper to taste. Garnish with cherry tomatoes.

Zucchini with Mustard Seeds or Cumin Seeds

3 or 4 small zucchini
1 tbsp. cooking oil (any kind)
½ tsp. mustard seeds or cumin seeds
¼ tsp. turmeric powder
Salt and pepper to taste

Dice zucchini into bite-size pieces. Heat oil in frying pan. Add mustard or cumin seeds, turmeric powder and zucchini. Cook till tender, about 10 to 15 minutes, or less if you prefer your zucchini crunchy. Add salt and pepper to taste. Remember that mustard seeds and cumin seeds each have a different flavor; use either one, or both.

Green Beans and Potatoes

Zucchini with Mustard Seeds

Cabbage and Potatoes

1 small cabbage, finely chopped
1 large potato, diced
½ tsp. cumin seeds
1 tbsp. cooking oil (any kind)
3 to 4 cloves of garlic, chopped
¼ tsp. turmeric powder
Salt and pepper to taste

Heat oil in frying pan. Add cumin seeds, garlic, turmeric powder, cabbage and potatoes. Cook till potatoes are tender, about 10 to 15 minutes. Salt and pepper to taste.

Hot Potato Salad

4 large potatoes, diced
½ tbsp. oil
⅛ tsp. mustard seeds
⅛ tsp. cumin seeds
⅛ tsp. turmeric powder
Pinch of asafoetida (heeng)
Salt to taste

Heat oil in pan, add mustard seeds, cumin seeds and asafoetida. When seeds pop, add potatoes, turmeric and salt. Cover pan and cook over medium flame for 10 to 12 minutes.

Fenugreek and Potatoes

Large bunch of fenugreek leaves, washed (remove stems)
2 large potatoes
4 cloves of garlic (or more, if desired)
⅛ tsp. turmeric
1 tbsp. oil

Peel the potatoes and dice into bite-size pieces. Heat oil in saucepan, add garlic, turmeric and potatoes, cook till fork-tender (about 10 minutes). Add fenugreek leaves, cook about 2 minutes. Serve as hot salad or side dish.

Brinjal (Eggplant) with Carom Seeds

1 large eggplant
2 small potatoes (optional)
¼ tsp. carom seeds
4 cloves of garlic
½ tsp. turmeric
Handful of coriander leaves
Lemon to taste
Salt and pepper (if desired)
1 tbsp. oil

Dice eggplant (and potato, if desired) into small pieces. Heat oil in frying pan, put in carom seeds. When seeds pop, add garlic and turmeric, then add eggplant and potatoes,(if desired); cook till eggplant is soft and potato is fork-tender (about 10 to 15 minutes). Add coriander, lemon, salt and pepper.

Yellow Moong Dal and Spring Onions

1 cup yellow moong dal, skinless, soaked for 2 or more hours
½ tsp. cumin seeds
¼ tsp. turmeric powder
6 or 7 spring onions, finely chopped
1 tbsp. oil
Salt and pepper to taste

Heat oil in skillet, put in cumin seeds and turmeric powder. Drain water from dal, put dal in skillet with a little water. Cook for 5 to 7 minutes over medium flame, till liquid dissolves. Remove from heat, add onions, salt and pepper, stir well.

Grilled Eggplant or Zucchini with Pomegranate Powder

1 large eggplant or 1 large zucchini, cut into ½ inch rounds
1 tbsp. oil (or more, if needed)
Powdered pomegranate seeds to taste
Salt and pepper to taste

Heat skillet, add eggplant, then oil as needed (eggplant will absorb oil, so don't add too much). Grill eggplant over medium heat till well-done (about 5 minutes). Add salt, pepper and powdered pomegranate seeds.

Pomegranate Seeds

Yellow Moong Dal and Spring Onions

Fenugreek Sprouts with Golden Raisins

½ cup fenugreek seeds (sprouted)
1 tbsp. oil
1 small onion, finely chopped
2 to 3 cloves of garlic, ground into paste
½ inch piece of ginger, ground into paste (see Chapter 12)
¼ cup of golden raisins
Pinch of turmeric
Salt and pepper to taste

Create sprouts from fenugreek seeds (see Chapter 3 for method). Heat oil, add onions, cook over medium flame till translucent. Add garlic and ginger paste, turmeric, salt and pepper. Then add raisins, mix well, cook 2 minutes. Remove from heat, then add sprouts. Serve hot.

Okra with Mustard Seeds and Pomegranate Powder

1 lb. okra (washed, wiped and diced)
2 tbsps. oil
1 tbsp. mustard seeds
2 or 3 curry leaves (if desired)
¼ tsp. turmeric
½ tsp. powdered pomegranate seeds
Salt and pepper to taste

Heat pan, add oil, then mustard seeds and curry leaves. When seeds pop, add okra and turmeric; lower flame. Cook okra till tender (about 10 mins.). Add salt and pepper and pomegranate seed powder. Serve hot.

Remember – once you add the seeds to the hot oil, wait till they pop, then add the other ingredients, so that you get the full flavor of the seeds. This is also the time to add crushed pepper, if desired. Cook over a low flame so that nothing burns and no flavor is lost.

Chapter Six
Squash

Squash, in all its many varieties, is one of the most useful and versatile of all vegetables, as well as one of the most nutritious. Since it contains vitamin A, it is a good anti-oxidant, and being high in potassium, it also helps to control blood pressure. Also, the fiber in squash helps the digestive system to function properly, which makes everything else work better, too.

I could not begin to list all the possible uses of squash, but here are a few suggestions:

⋆ Fresh, tender, grated squash (any kind of squash that can be eaten raw) mixed with yogurt makes a delicious, cold side dish (to season the yogurt, heat a teaspoon of oil in a pan, then add a pinch each of mustard seeds, cumin seeds, crushed pepper and asafoetida (heeng), and mix it with the yogurt).

⋆ Sprinkle grated squash on top of your favorite salad.

⋆ Stir-fry chopped squash with your favorite spices.

⋆ Steamed or baked: cut squash in half, drizzle with butter or oil, season with your favorite spices (toasted and crushed).

⋆ Mix diced squash into almost any soup.

⋆ Steamed and puréed squash makes a great meal for a child.

My own favorite use for squash is to make Spaghetti Squash Pudding. (I remember my mother making rice pudding in wintertime, and squash pudding in summertime.)

Here is the basic recipe for Spaghetti Squash Pudding:

3 cups milk
Half of a fresh green summer squash (any kind of squash will do; my favorite is spaghetti squash, but it must be used while the skin is still soft and green, not yellow)
2 cinnamon sticks
2 or 3 cardamom pods
Pinch of saffron
Pinch of nutmeg
Sugar to taste
Raisins or nuts, if desired

Peel the cardamom pods and crush them with a rolling pin to create a powder. Scrape skin from squash, then grate the squash into a bowl, set aside. Put milk into saucepan, bring to a boil. Lower flame, add all the spices, let boil about 15 to 20 minutes, stirring constantly. Add squash to milk and spice mixture, cook over medium heat until desired thickness is achieved. Add sugar to taste, and raisins or nuts, if desired. Remove cinnamon sticks before serving.

In my little back yard, which is hardly 10′ X 10′, I have learned to grow my own squash. It is softer and fresher than the squash from the market. If you're interested (and you have the time and the space), growing your own will make the whole squash experience even more enjoyable!

One last point about squash: it can only be used for pudding while the skin is soft (this is known as summer squash). When the skin turns hard, it is called winter squash, and can be used for savory dishes, such as soups, bakes, stir-fries, etc.

Ingredients used in Squash Recipe

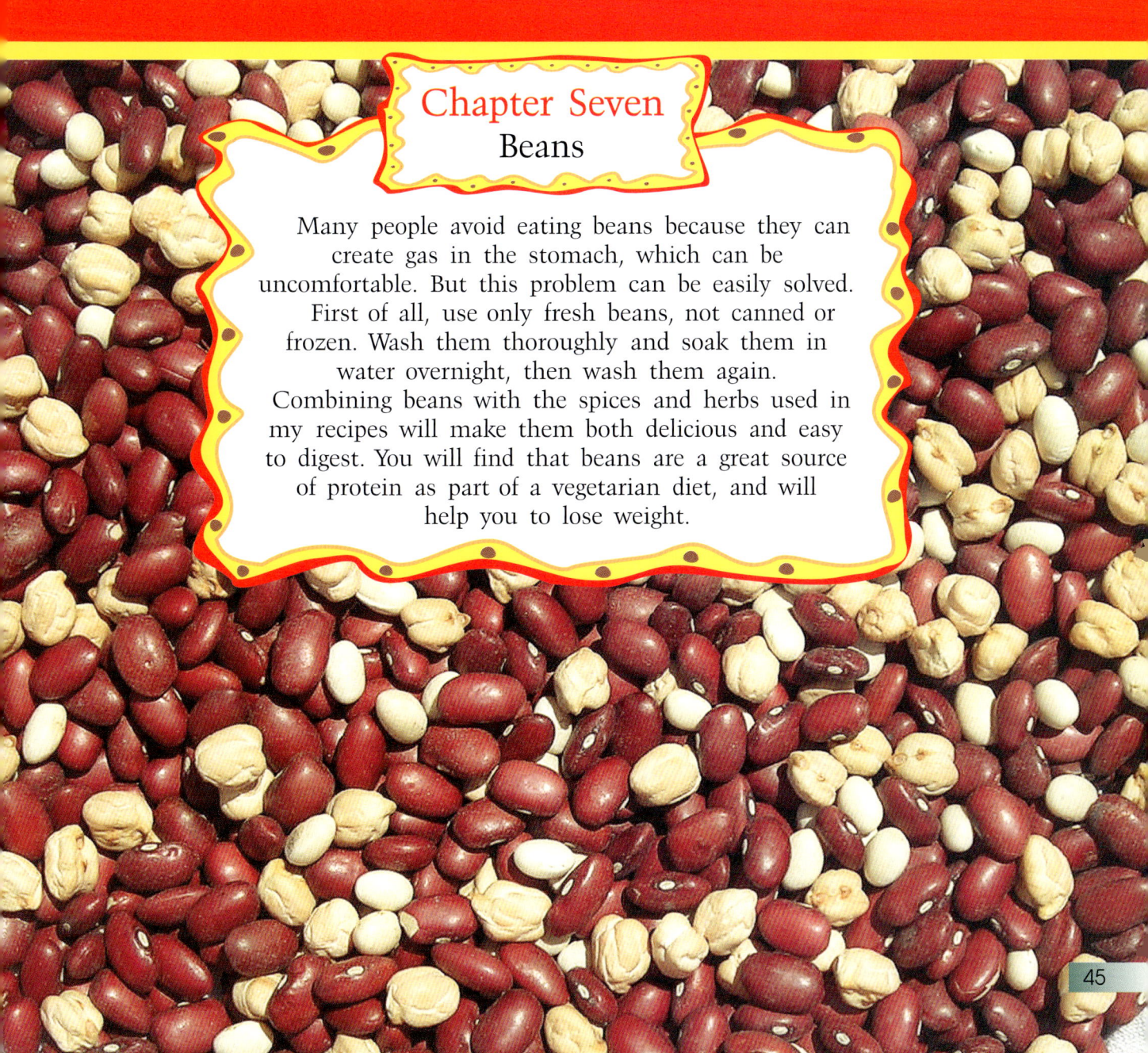

Chapter Seven
Beans

Many people avoid eating beans because they can create gas in the stomach, which can be uncomfortable. But this problem can be easily solved. First of all, use only fresh beans, not canned or frozen. Wash them thoroughly and soak them in water overnight, then wash them again. Combining beans with the spices and herbs used in my recipes will make them both delicious and easy to digest. You will find that beans are a great source of protein as part of a vegetarian diet, and will help you to lose weight.

Red Kidney Beans with Onion and Tomato

1 large onion, finely chopped
1 large tomato, finely chopped
⅛ tsp. turmeric
⅛ tsp. carom seeds
⅛ tsp. celery seeds
⅛ tsp. cumin seeds
1 tsp. garlic and ginger paste (see Chapter 12)
1 cup red kidney beans, washed, soaked overnight
1 tbsp. oil
Salt and pepper to taste
Water (as needed)
Cilantro, if desired as a garnish

Heat oil in pan. Add all the seeds; when they pop, add onions, cook till translucent, add garlic and ginger paste, turmeric, salt and pepper, tomatoes. When the oil rises to the top, add beans; add enough water to come to an inch over the beans. Bring to boil, lower flame, cook till beans are done (1 to 2 hrs.). Garnish with cilantro if you wish.

If you are using a pressure cooker, use the same directions as above, follow the instructions for your particular pressure cooker, and you can remove beans from heat after about 30 minutes.

Red Kidney Beans with Onion and Tomato

Chapter Eight
Sauces

The word "curry" in Indian cooking does not refer to any one particular flavor, it simply means any sauce or gravy. The Hindi term "tar kari", meaning a dish containing solid food floating in a liquid, is the origin of the English word "curry". Whichever word you prefer, here are a few of my favorites. These sauces are very versatile; how you use them is up to you.

Onion and Tomato-Based Curry

1 large onion, finely chopped
1 large tomato, finely chopped
⅛ tsp. cumin seeds
1 tsp. ground garlic and ginger paste (see Chapter 12)
⅛ tsp. turmeric
Salt and pepper to taste
Chopped cilantro (if desired)
1 tbsp. oil

Heat the oil in a saucepan over a medium flame. Add cumin seeds, let seeds pop, add onions. When onions become translucent, add garlic and ginger paste, mix well, then add turmeric, salt and pepper and tomatoes. Cook over low flame till sauce becomes thick, and oil rises to the top (2 to 3 minutes). Now you can add your favorite vegetables. You can have this just as it is, with bread or rolls, crackers, etc.

Once you have made the sauce, you can add heavy cream, yogurt or coconut milk to make three different sauces, or add water to create gravy. A variation on this sauce is as follows: in addition to the ingredients listed above, add cinnamon powder, clove powder and a pinch of nutmeg for a very unusual and special flavor.
It makes a great sauce for chick peas. Sometimes I add cubes of paneer (cottage cheese) and sliced bell pepper to the sauce.

Coconut Curry

1 can of coconut milk (13.5 ounces)
2 tsps. fennel seeds
1 tsp. white poppy seeds
2 or 3 cloves
1 small onion, finely chopped
1 small tomato, finely chopped
2 to 4 cloves of garlic
Small piece of ginger (½ inch), if desired
4 curry leaves
½ tsp. oil
⅛ tsp. turmeric powder
Salt and pepper to taste
Pinch of grated nutmeg
⅛ tsp. powdered cinnamon
5 or 6 stems of cilantro, finely chopped

In a dry frying pan, toast fennel seeds, poppy seeds and cloves, then grind in coffee grinder. Heat oil in pan, add garlic and ginger, curry leaves, onion, cinnamon and nutmeg, cook over low flame till it becomes pinkish-brown. Put this in a blender, add coconut milk and ground seed mix, then add tomatoes. Blend into a thick mixture (about 1 minute). Put oil into pan, add chopped cilantro; after a few seconds, add turmeric powder, salt and pepper, then pour in sauce mix from blender. Bring to boil, add your favorite vegetables, cook them in the sauce.

Curry Leaves

White Poppy Seed Sauce

2 tbsps. white poppy seeds, soaked for 1 hour, then finely ground (stone grind for best results)
1 small onion, finely chopped
4 cloves of garlic
Salt and white pepper to taste
Water, as desired
2 tsps. oil
Juice of ½ lemon, or more or less to taste
⅛ tsp. mustard seeds

Heat 1 tsp. oil in frying pan over low flame, add garlic and onions, cook till pinkish-brown; remove from heat. Put this in blender, add ground poppy seeds, lemon juice, salt and pepper. Blend to thickness of a milk shake, or as thick as desired. (Remember, poppy seed is a thickening agent.) Put 1 tsp. oil in pan, add mustard seeds; when seeds pop, pour in sauce, cook over low flame for about 5 minutes.

When I was a kid, we would usually have this sauce with rice and fried fish on the side. This was one of my grandma's favorite recipes.

If you prefer, you can use red pepper, red chilli powder or paprika instead of black pepper (except in the white poppy seed sauce).

Chapter Nine
Fries

Regular Fries (Fritters)

Potatoes/Eggplant/Zucchini/Cauliflower/Bell Pepper/Squash Flowers
6 to 10 tsps. gram flour
1/8 tsp. carom seeds
1/8 tsp. fennel seeds
Pinch of asafoetida (heeng)
Salt to taste
Any cooking oil
Water

Slice potatoes, eggplant or zucchini into rounds. Separate cauliflower into florets. Cut bell pepper into 4 to 6 pieces. All vegetables must be washed and patted dry.

Mix flour, carom seeds, fennel seeds and asafoetida with enough water to create a thick consistency. Put oil into frying pan, heat over medium flame for about 5 minutes. Put a teaspoon of hot oil into the batter. Put a few pieces of vegetables into batter, mix well, place carefully into hot oil.

Cook over medium flame till golden brown (2 to 4 minutes).
Remove from oil, drain on paper towels. Serve hot. You can have the fries with chutney, yogurt/mint dip or relish, but if they turn out right, you don't need anything else but a cup of hot tea or lemonade.

Moong Dal Fries

Moong Dal Fries

1 cup of skinless split moong dal, soaked for at least 2 hrs.
Cooking oil
¼ tsp. cumin seeds
Pinch of asafoetida (heeng)
¼ tsp. coriander seeds, crushed (optional)
Salt and pepper to taste
Sliced ginger (optional)

Put dal into food processor (with ginger, if desired), grind coarsely. Mix dal with cumin seeds, coriander seeds and asafoetida. With a teaspoon, place small amounts of dal mixture into hot oil. Cook till golden brown (2 to 4 minutes). Drain on paper towels. Serve hot.

Potato Fritters

2 large potatoes
Gram flour
⅛ tsp. carom seeds
Pinch of asafoetida (heeng)
Salt and pepper to taste
Cooking oil

Peel, wash and grate potatoes, add carom seeds, asafoetida, salt and pepper, mix thoroughly, then add gram flour, stir till batter is thick and smooth. Heat oil in pan, then add a little hot oil to the batter; mix well. Place desired amount of batter into hot oil, according to the size of fritter you want. Cook over medium flame till golden brown (about 2 to 3 minutes on each side). Drain on paper towels. Serve with applesauce, yogurt, ketchup, or any chutney or relish.
Enjoy with tea, coffee or lemonade.

In addition to all this, you can make fries with squash, zucchini and pumpkin flowers, and the tender leaves of pumpkin and squash, as well as basil and mint leaves.
Just make sure that the batter for these fries is a little thinner than usual, so that you do not overpower the flavor of the leaves and the flowers.
With all these fries, you can be a bit naughty without doing yourself any harm.

Chapter Ten
Roti

ROTI (Unleavened Indian Bread)

Bread is an essential part of almost every national cuisine, and a delicious helping of fresh, hot bread makes a meal complete. Indian bread is known as roti. It is an element of Indian cooking that is beloved by almost everyone of any age.

Here is the basic method for making rotis:

Mix 2 cups of whole wheat flour together with 1 cup of water (use more water if needed). Knead by hand for about a minute, or use a food processor to make dough. Add about ½ tsp. oil to dough – this will make it easier to handle. Let dough rest for a couple of minutes. Break off a small piece of dough and form it into a ball, then use a rolling pin to flatten it out. Heat a non-stick pan over a high flame, then lower flame, place the flat piece of dough on the pan, count ten and turn it over. Cook about ½ minute, turn it again, then press gently with a cloth or small towel till the roti puffs up; remove from heat with pincers (watch the steam!). This can be varied by including in the dough carom seeds, ground sprouts, or almost any leftover vegetables (just grind them in a food processor). You can also create delicious stuffed breads! Just grind vegetables in a food processor, then add them to the flour when making the dough (you may or may not need water, depending on how moist the vegetables are).

For roti stuffed with potato, you just put a little oil on the roti dough, add a couple of spoonfuls of mashed potato, fold over the edges of the roti, roll it out again, and cook as usual.

The dough can be kept for 2 to 3 days in the fridge. Rotis can be enjoyed plain, or with butter, cheese, jelly, egg, or countless other spreads or fillings. And you can make them in whatever size, shape or thickness you prefer.

Chapter Eleven
Chai

Tea drinking is so important an element of Indian life that even shepherds and cattle herders in the most far-off plains and mountains brew their evening cup of chai over an open fire.

The different varieties of chai, and their many medicinal uses, may come as a surprise if you think of tea only as a soothing beverage. It is that, of course, but it is so much more.

Among the many spices that can be used to flavor a cup of chai, some of the most popular are cinnamon, cardamom, ginger, clove, mint and anise. I have included several basic chai recipes, but you can experiment with different combinations and amounts to find the formulas that best suit your taste.

The health benefits of tea drinking have been known in India for thousands of years. A tea made from dill seeds is traditionally used for one month after childbirth. The mother drinks it as a means of cleansing the system. This can be taken either hot or cold.

In addition, a recent study has concluded that people who drink tea regularly (one cup or more per day) have a much lower risk of developing the two most common forms of skin cancer. The study also found that if one remains a steady tea drinker over a period of years, the cancer risk continues to decrease.

A soothing beverage - Tea (Chai)

Basic Tea Recipes

Milk Chai (Milk Tea)

Put one cup water and one cup milk into saucepan, turn on heat, add ¼ inch piece of ginger, 1 clove, 1 cardamom seed, ⅛ tsp. anise seeds (crush all seeds for more flavor), one small piece of cinnamon, bring to boil. Add 2 tsps. tea leaves (more or less according to taste). Lower flame, simmer one minute. Strain, then add sugar or honey to taste.

Black Tea

Put 2 cups water into pan, bring to boil. Add ⅛ inch piece of ginger and 1 crushed cardamom seed. Lower flame, boil 1 minute. Add ½ tsp. tea leaves, simmer ½ minute. Strain, then add lemon if desired. Sweeten to taste.

Mint Tea

Put 2 to 2½ cups water into pan, bring to boil. Break 10 to 15 mint leaves into water. Lower flame, boil 1 minute. Add ¼ tsp. tea leaves, boil 1 minute more. Serve hot or cold.

Lemongrass Tea

¼ tsp. tea leaves or 1 teabag, one 1-inch piece of lemongrass, or one 6-inch lemongrass leaf

Put lemongrass into 2 to 2½ cups of water; bring to boil. Lower flame, simmer for 2 to 3 minutes. Add tea leaves and boil 1 minute or to desired strength, or dip tea bag to obtain desired strength. Add sugar, honey or lemon if desired.

Mint Lemonade

Juice of 4 to 6 lemons
1 quart water
Handful of mint leaves
Sugar to taste
Ice

Combine all the ingredients in a blender. Blend till leaves are fine and ice is crushed. Refrigerate. (This is not a tea, of course, but you will find that it is one of the most cooling, refreshing and soothing drinks you can enjoy on a hot summer day.)

Iced Tea

Put 4 to 6 cups water into pan, bring to boil. Add ½ inch piece of ginger, 2 cinnamon sticks, lemon peel, 2 cloves. Lower flame, boil 5 minutes. Add 1 tsp. tea leaves, boil 1 minute more. Strain, sweeten to taste, let cool for about 15 to 20 minutes, put in refrigerator till cold.

Each of the spices I have mentioned can be used separately to create a delicious cup of tea, with or without milk. I suggest you do not combine milk and lemon, but any other combination of these ingredients will work beautifully. (If you prefer, you can use tea bags instead of loose tea leaves. Just boil the water with your favorite spices, then dip the tea bag to obtain the desired strength.)

Chapter Twelve
Tips

+ For garlic and ginger paste, use three parts garlic to one part ginger; grind in a food processor for about a minute. It will keep in the fridge for seven to ten days, if necessary.

+ When using ginger in soup, you can either grate it or place a whole piece into the pot, but remember to remove the piece before serving the dish.

+ If you cannot eat salt or prefer not to, you can replace it with lemon, lime, pomegranate seed powder, lemon powder (found in Persian markets) or mango powder. Try them all and see; they are all delicious.

+ A nursing mother and a growing child can both eat dal. As the child grows, add potato, squash, pumpkin, peas, beans or any other vegetable to the dal. Mother and child can share the same meal!

+ When using mustard seeds, cumin seeds, etc. in a recipe, after you put them into the hot oil, always wait till they pop before adding any other ingredients. This will bring out their full flavor.

+ Carom seeds, ginger and asafoetida (also called heeng) are all useful for counteracting gas.

+ All dals are excellent for preventing or treating anemia, since they have a very high iron content. They are also full of protein, and will help you to lose weight.

+ When I mention "pepper" in these recipes, it doesn't just mean black pepper. You can use any kind of pepper you like (red pepper flakes, red chilli powder, green chillies). Find out what suits your taste.

+ Avoid putting turmeric in your blender, because it will turn the inside of the blender yellow.

+ Once you become familiar with the various spices, you can create a delicious seasoning by toasting your favorite spices, combining them in any way you like, and then grinding them into a powder in a coffee grinder. This will be great for sprinkling on stews, soups, vegetables, etc. (While your baby has plain, unseasoned soup, you can enjoy the same soup, but seasoned exactly to your taste!) You will find it a lot easier to cook with spices if you store them all together in one holder (masala dabba). That way, they will all be handy, and you won't burn your oil while you are trying to find the right spice.

+ The spices in my recipes are so flavorful that you don't need to add much salt and pepper; so if you prefer not to use them, you will still get the full flavor of the dishes.

+ Remember: always listen to your own body -- it will tell you what it wants and needs, as well as what it doesn't want or need. It is a gift from God, and must be taken care of.

Chapter Thirteen
Medicinal Values

Asafoetida(Heeng): Relieves stomach ache and gas; repels insects

Basil: Helps you to sleep (add to boiling water)

Cardamom: Eases digestion

Cinnamon: Prevents bad breath; useful against upset stomach; reduces blood sugar; medication for cold (simmer cinnamon sticks and cloves for 3 minutes, strain, add 2 tsps. lemon juice and 2 tsps. honey)

Clove: Relieves pain of toothache and sore gums; relieves bad breath; eases cough (put a whole clove in the mouth)

Dill: Dill seeds in boiling water ease insomnia; combine with anise, caraway and coriander to stimulate flow of milk in nursing mothers; chewing seeds relieves bad breath

Fennel: Fennel tea sweetens mother's milk and relieves colic; chewing seeds relieves bad breath

Fenugreek: Fenugreek tea relieves colic; reduces cholesterol; helps digestion

Masala Dabba

Garlic: Useful as an antibiotic; destroys internal parasites; reduces cholesterol; repels insects

Ginger: Ginger tea is useful against nausea and congestion. Ginger in any form is helpful against the pain of arthritis

Mint: Mint tea eases headache, stomach ache, heartburn and cramp

Turmeric: Anti-oxidant; powdered turmeric can speed healing of sores, bruises and wounds; anti-inflammatory; regular use of turmeric is also believed to inhibit the onset of Alzheimer's disease and other similar conditions

Remember -- These ancient remedies are not meant to take the place of modern medications. But they have been healing the human race for thousands of years, and should never be forgotten. The most important thing to remember is that all spices improve digestion, and that will improve your total health.

Mint and Ginger

Chapter Fourteen
A Final Word

The recipes in this little book are not meant only for special occasions; they are for everyday use. Not all days can be Christmas or Thanksgiving. But it's my hope that the dishes I have presented will help turn everyday meals into occasions that are at least somewhat special.

You will find that once you have become familiar with the spices I have mentioned, you can create an unlimited variety of sauces, soups, stews, entrées and side dishes simply by varying and combining them in any way that pleases you. What I have provided are only the ABC's of spices; the rest is up to you. Let your imagination go – using spices will open the door to a new world of flavor and fun. But don't let the spices overpower the food; learn to use the right amounts.

Another way to enhance your enjoyment of cookery is to team up with friends and become what I call "cooking buddies". Share your culinary ideas and experiences with each other, and venture forth together to explore any new and different ethnic markets that happen to be nearby.

Ask questions; you may be fascinated by what you learn.

It isn't difficult to prepare fresh food every day. It's just a matter of planning. Plan your shopping so that you have enough good grains on hand at all times, make your sprouts so that you have them ready seven days a week, and then you'll be able to have a delicious soup or salad in no time. Once you become familiar with the ingredients I have introduced you to, you'll be surprised to see just how simple it all is, and what a big difference they make in your total health.

God has given us the beautiful gift of the human body. Learn to take care of it. We should eat to live, not live to eat. Remember that health is wealth.

I have found that the simplest things in life are often the most beautiful. Learn to enjoy them.

As I have spiced up my life, you can spice up yours!

A Final Word

In this book I have given you some examples of how turmeric can be used in a variety of recipes. But this is only the beginning. Now that you understand how turmeric can be used in cooking, you can start to create your own dishes using the King of Spices. These recipes are not hard and fast rules, feel free to alter them any way you like to produce your own creations! Once you make turmeric a part of your life, you may be amazed at what it can do for your general health. Not only can it help to clear up numerous physical conditions that may be troubling you, but it can also prevent further problems from ever developing. Turmeric will bring color to your table, and by improving your health and thus increasing your happiness, turmeric can truly bring color into your life.

Bow Tie Pasta with Snow Peas

Spaghetti with Parsley

½ lb. spaghetti
Handful of mushrooms
Handful of parsley
2 or 3 cloves of garlic, crushed
Olive oil
Salt and pepper to taste
Pinch of turmeric

Make spaghetti as usual, set aside.
Heat oil in skillet over medium flame.
Add garlic and turmeric, wait a few
seconds, then add mushrooms.
After a minute or so, add parsley,
mix well for about a minute. Mix in
spaghetti; add salt and pepper to taste.

Bow Tie Pasta with Snow Peas

½ lb. bow tie pasta
1 handful of snow peas, with
strings removed
1 large onion, diced
2 tbsps. olive oil
8 to 10 cherry tomatoes
4 to 6 medium-sized mushrooms, sliced
¼ tsp. turmeric powder
4 to 6 cloves of garlic, sliced or crushed
Salt and pepper to taste

Prepare pasta as usual, set aside. Heat
pan over medium flame, lower flame,
add oil and onions. When onions
become translucent, add garlic, stir,
add turmeric. Stir in snow peas; cook
for a minute, add mushrooms and
pasta; stir well and cook for a minute
or two. Remove from heat; add cherry
tomatoes. Cover for a minute or so
before serving.

Pasta with Ground Turkey

1 lb. ground turkey
1 tbsp. oil
½ tsp. carom seeds
¼ tsp. turmeric powder
1 large onion, finely chopped
4 to 6 cloves of garlic, to taste
Two 8 oz. cans of tomato sauce,
or 4 large tomatoes, chopped
and blended
Salt and pepper to taste

To make the sauce:
heat deep pan
over medium heat,
add oil and
carom seeds;
when seeds pop,
add onion.

When onion becomes translucent,
add garlic, turmeric and ground turkey,
stir well. Cook over medium heat
for 10 minutes, add tomato sauce,
cook for 10 to 15 minutes till turkey
is fully cooked. You can vary this by
adding celery and carrots, and leaving
out the carom seeds.

Cook pasta as usual, mix with sauce.
If you prefer,
you can
simply add
¼ tsp. of
turmeric into
the boiling
pasta water,
and get your
turmeric
that way!

Ground Turkey with Peas and Cherry Tomatoes

½ pound ground turkey
1 medium-sized onion, finely chopped
1 tbsp. oil
3 to 4 cloves of garlic
1 cup peas, fresh or frozen
10 cherry tomatoes
Pinch of turmeric
Salt and pepper to taste

Heat skillet or wok over medium heat, add oil and onion. When onion becomes translucent, add garlic and stir.

Add turmeric and ground turkey, mix well, lower flame and cover. Cook for about 15 to 20 minutes. Add peas, cover and cook for a minute or so, depending on how tender you like your peas. Remove from heat and add tomatoes.

This is an excellent side dish, but if you want to turn it into a main meal, just dice one large potato and add it along with the ground turkey.

Ground Turkey Meatballs

Ground Turkey Meatballs

Meatballs:

1 to 1½ pounds ground turkey
1 tbsp. thyme
Salt and pepper to taste
Pinch of turmeric

Sauce:

4 to 6 large tomatoes, crushed or
blended in a blender
1 medium-sized onion, finely chopped
2 celery stalks, thinly sliced
1 tbsp. thyme
Handful of basil leaves, washed
and crumbled
Salt and pepper to taste
Pinch of turmeric
1 tbsp. olive oil
4 to 6 cloves of garlic

Put ground turkey, thyme, salt and pepper and turmeric into a mixing bowl; mix well and set aside. In a large pot, heat oil over medium flame.

Add onions and celery, when onions become translucent, add turmeric, garlic, basil leaves, tomato sauce and thyme, lower flame, let simmer till it boils.

Make meatballs by taking a teaspoon (or more if you prefer) of the ground turkey and forming it into a ball between your palms. Place each one into the sauce. (There will be about 20 meatballs, depending on their size.)

Cover pot and cook for about 20 minutes. Don't stir with a spoon, just move the pot around a few times while the meatballs are cooking. The meatballs can be served with pasta or rice, or made into hero sandwiches.

Rice Pilaf with Chicken

1 cup rice
2 chicken legs with thighs,
washed and skinned
1 small onion, finely chopped
Garlic and ginger paste
Pinch of turmeric
Pinch of nutmeg
1 tbsp. oil
Salt, pepper and lemon to taste
2 cups water

Heat oil in large pot over a high flame, then lower flame and add onions. When onions become translucent, put in garlic and ginger paste, turmeric, nutmeg, salt and pepper. Put chicken into pot and roast it for about 10 minutes on each side. Raise the flame, add rice, mix well and add water. When water boils, give a quick stir, lower flame, cover pot and cook for 20 minutes. Serve hot, garnish with greens if you like.

Flounder with Garlic and Parsley

2 flounder fillets
3 to 4 cloves of garlic
Pinch of turmeric
Handful of parsley
Juice of 2 lemons or 2 limes
3 tsps. olive oil
Salt and pepper to taste

Heat a large skillet over medium flame, add oil and garlic. When garlic is golden-brown, add turmeric, lower flame and let it cook for about a minute. Add lemon or lime juice, parsley, and salt to taste, then put in flounder fillets. Turn them over immediately so that both sides will be coated with the garlic-oil-turmeric-parsley mixture. Cover skillet and cook over medium flame for 15 to 20 minutes.

You can also make a delicious steamed flounder dish by taking 2 flounder fillets, rolling them up and securing them with toothpicks. Then put them in a steamer for about 20 to 30 minutes. If you don't have a steamer, use a skillet with about half a cup of water seasoned with lemon or vinegar and a drop of oil. Boil the water, put in the fish, and cover the skillet. Lower flame and cook for about 10 to 15 minutes. Remove fish with slotted spoon, put on serving dish, and cover the fish with the lima bean sauce (refer to page 5), with a little butter mixed into the dip.

Stuffed Flounder

2 flounder fillets
2 spring onions
½ leek
6 to 8 mushrooms
Handful of spinach, chopped,
washed and dried
2 to 3-inch piece of fresh white
turmeric (or ¼ tsp. turmeric powder)
2 cloves of garlic
1 tsp. bread crumbs (optional)
4 tsps. oil
2 tsps. Parmesan cheese
Salt and pepper to taste

Heat oil in skillet over medium flame. Dice mushrooms, leeks, onions and turmeric into small pieces, put into oil. Cook over low flame for about 10 minutes, then add spinach, cook for another minute or two, stir in bread crumbs (if you like) and remove from heat. Wash flounder fillets and pat dry. Put 3 to 4 tablespoons of vegetable stuffing onto each fillet. Roll them up and secure with a toothpick.
Brush a little oil in a pan or baking dish, put in fish, bake for 20 to 25 minutes at 450 degrees. Remove toothpicks, sprinkle with Parmesan cheese and bake for another few seconds till cheese melts.

**Poached Salmon
with Yu Choy
and Spinach**

Poached Salmon

2 salmon fillets (about ½ lb. each)
1 cup cold water
Pinch of turmeric
Dash of lemon
Pinch of salt

Wash salmon. Put water, turmeric, lemon and salt in a skillet. Add salmon, cook over high flame till liquid boils. Lower flame and cover skillet. Cook for 20 to 30 minutes, depending on how you like your salmon.
(The salmon will absorb the water, and the fish will cook in its own oil.)

Poached Salmon with Yu Choy and Spinach

2 salmon fillets (about ½ lb. each)
1 large bunch of spinach
1 large bunch of yu choy
2 cloves of garlic, sliced
2 to 3 tsps. oil
Pinch of turmeric
Juice of ½ lemon
Salt to taste

Yu Choy

Wash spinach and remove stems, wash yu choy. Wash salmon, rub with turmeric, lemon and salt, put aside. Heat oil over high flame in deep skillet. Add garlic, cook till it becomes light brown (about a minute). Stir spinach and yu choy into oil, move greens to one side of skillet, then put salmon on other side of skillet. The salmon will absorb all the water from the greens. When it all begins to bubble, lower the flame and cover the skillet; cook for 20 to 30 minutes till cooked through. Serve immediately, with the salmon resting on a bed of greens.

Grilled Salmon

1 large salmon fillet (about 1 lb.)
Pinch of turmeric
Juice of 1 lemon, to taste
Salt to taste
½ tsp. to 1 tsp. oil

Marinate salmon in lemon juice, turmeric and salt for at least an hour. Heat grill pan over high heat, add oil.

When pan is very hot, put in salmon and reduce heat to medium. Cook for about 3 to 5 minutes on each side (this is approximate; cooking time depends on your own taste). If you like, you can finish it up in the oven for a couple of minutes at about 350 degrees. Serve with raw or steamed vegetables, as you like.

Shrimp with Three-Grain Pilaf

1 lb. of shrimp, cleaned and de-veined
1 medium-sized onion, finely chopped
1 medium-sized tomato, diced
4 to 6 cloves of garlic
Pinch of turmeric
½ cup grain mixture (cracked wheat, quinoa, millet)
1 tbsp. cooking oil
2 or 3 tsps. olive oil
2 cups of water
Salt and pepper to taste
Cilantro or parsley to garnish

Heat saucepan, heat grain mixture over low flame, about 3 to 4 minutes till toasted (the aroma will tell you), add 1 cup water, raise flame, bring to boil, lower flame as much as possible.
Cover and cook for 20 minutes. Add olive oil; stir well. Salt to taste.
(If you like, you can add raisins, nuts or onions, along with a little extra olive oil, for a delicious grain salad!)

In a skillet or wok, heat oil over medium flame. Slice garlic, add to oil, let garlic brown, add onion; when onion becomes translucent, add shrimp and turmeric, mix well. Let simmer for 2 minutes, add tomatoes, salt and pepper, cover, cook over low flame for about 5 minutes (more or less to taste). Garnish with parsley or cilantro.

Fried Fish and Shrimps

This little story seems appropriate here:

When I was about 10 years old, we lived on a small farm and had no refrigerator. One day, a friend of ours went fishing and caught some big ones. They were more than he could use, so he gave one to us. This was late at night, so in order to preserve the fish to use in the morning, my mother cleaned it and rubbed it thoroughly with a mixture of turmeric and salt. Next day, she cut up the fish. Some of it we fried, some was used to make curry, and the head was used for soup.
We all loved it!
Just another of the many amazing uses of turmeric.

Mix all ingredients together in a bowl till it becomes a nice, thick paste. If you feel like adding a little water, it's OK, but it shouldn't be necessary. Rub the marinade into each piece of fish; with shrimp, see that all pieces are well-coated. This will keep in the fridge for about three days.

(If you prefer to grill your fish or shrimp rather than fry it, just leave out the flour.)

Recently I did some cooking for a group of home-schooled children who were learning about India, along with their parents. I prepared fried fish using marinade number 2 above, and everybody loved it, especially the kids!

Fried Fish or Shrimp

To fry your marinated fish or shrimp, you can use bread crumbs, farina or panco. Put a cup of crumbs on a plate; place a piece of marinated fish or shrimp on top, then turn it to coat the other side. Make sure it is all well-coated. Put about 1 cup of oil in a shallow frying pan, heat oil over high flame. When oil is hot, lower flame to medium, and carefully put in fish. Cook about 3 to 5 minutes on each side (according to taste). The shrimp should cook for about 1 minute on each side, or less if preferred.

Stir-fried Shrimp

Stir-fried Shrimp

*1 lb. of shrimp, cleaned and
de-veined
1 tbsp. cooking oil
1 tsp. garlic and ginger paste (or just
2 to 3 crushed cloves of garlic,
if you prefer)
Pinch of turmeric
Salt and pepper to taste
Dash of lemon juice, if desired*

Heat wok over medium flame for about
a minute, then put in oil, garlic and
ginger paste (or just garlic) and
turmeric, then add shrimp. Keep
stirring; lower flame if you wish.
In about 2 or 3 minutes, it will be
ready. Add salt, pepper and lemon to
your taste.
This can be enjoyed as a side dish, or
you can make it part of a salad.
It is great hot or cold!

If you want to have it as a main dish,
just add one large onion, sliced or diced
as you like it. Put in the onion right
after the oil (put in a little extra oil);
when onion becomes translucent,
continue recipe as above. When it's
ready, garnish with parsley,
cilantro or mint.
Enjoy it with bread, rice or pasta.

Marinades for Fried Seafood

These can be used with shrimp,
halibut, flounder, sea bass, tilapia,
or almost any fish.

1.   *½ tsp. turmeric powder
     Juice of one lemon
     1 tsp. whole wheat flour
     Salt to taste*

2.   *1 tsp. garlic and ginger paste
     ¼ tsp. turmeric
     1 tsp. tamarind, or juice of
     one lemon or lime (you can
     also add the zest)
     2 tsps. whole wheat flour or
     chick pea flour
     Salt and pepper to taste*

Sesame Seed Dip

Sesame Seed Dip

½ cup sesame seeds
1 to 2 cloves of garlic
Pinch of powdered turmeric or
½-inch piece of fresh turmeric,
finely chopped
2 or 3 teaspoons yogurt or dash of
olive oil and lemon, as you prefer
Salt and pepper to taste

Dry-grind the sesame seeds in a coffee grinder. In a food processor, put sesame seeds, garlic, yogurt (or olive oil and lemon), and pulse it a few times.
Put into serving bowl, garnish with fresh turmeric.
This will give you a white-colored dip. If you don't have fresh turmeric, or if you want a cream-colored dip, put the powdered turmeric into the food processor along with the other ingredients.

Hummus

½ cup chick peas (soaked overnight)
½ cup dry-ground sesame seeds
Juice of one lemon or lime
Garlic to taste
1 to 2 tbsps. olive oil
Pinch of turmeric
Paprika to taste
Salt to taste

Wash chick peas. Boil in enough water to cover for about
30 minutes, or use pressure cooker (follow manufacturer's directions).
Put chick peas into food processor, pulse a few times, add ground sesame seeds, then all other ingredients except olive oil; mix well, then add olive oil, grind to paste consistency (about a minute).

Turmeric Relish

*2 or 3 one-inch pieces of both white
and yellow turmeric, thinly sliced
or shredded
Dash of lemon juice
Salt to taste*

Mix all ingredients together in a bowl.
Can be used with fish, salads, or
almost any food.

Lima Bean Dip

*1 cup lima beans
1 to 2 tsps. olive oil
1 one-inch piece of white turmeric
1 one-inch piece of yellow turmeric
Salt to taste*

Wash the beans and soak them
overnight. Remove skin (don't worry;
it will come off easily). Cook the
beans for about 30 minutes in enough
water to cover them, or use pressure
cooker (follow manufacturer's directions).
Mash the beans with
a potato masher or
fork; slice turmeric
into small pieces and
mix into beans along
with olive oil.
Garnish with any
kind of greens if you
wish. To make the
dip into a sauce,
just add a little
extra water and
some butter to
desired consistency!

Lima Bean Dip

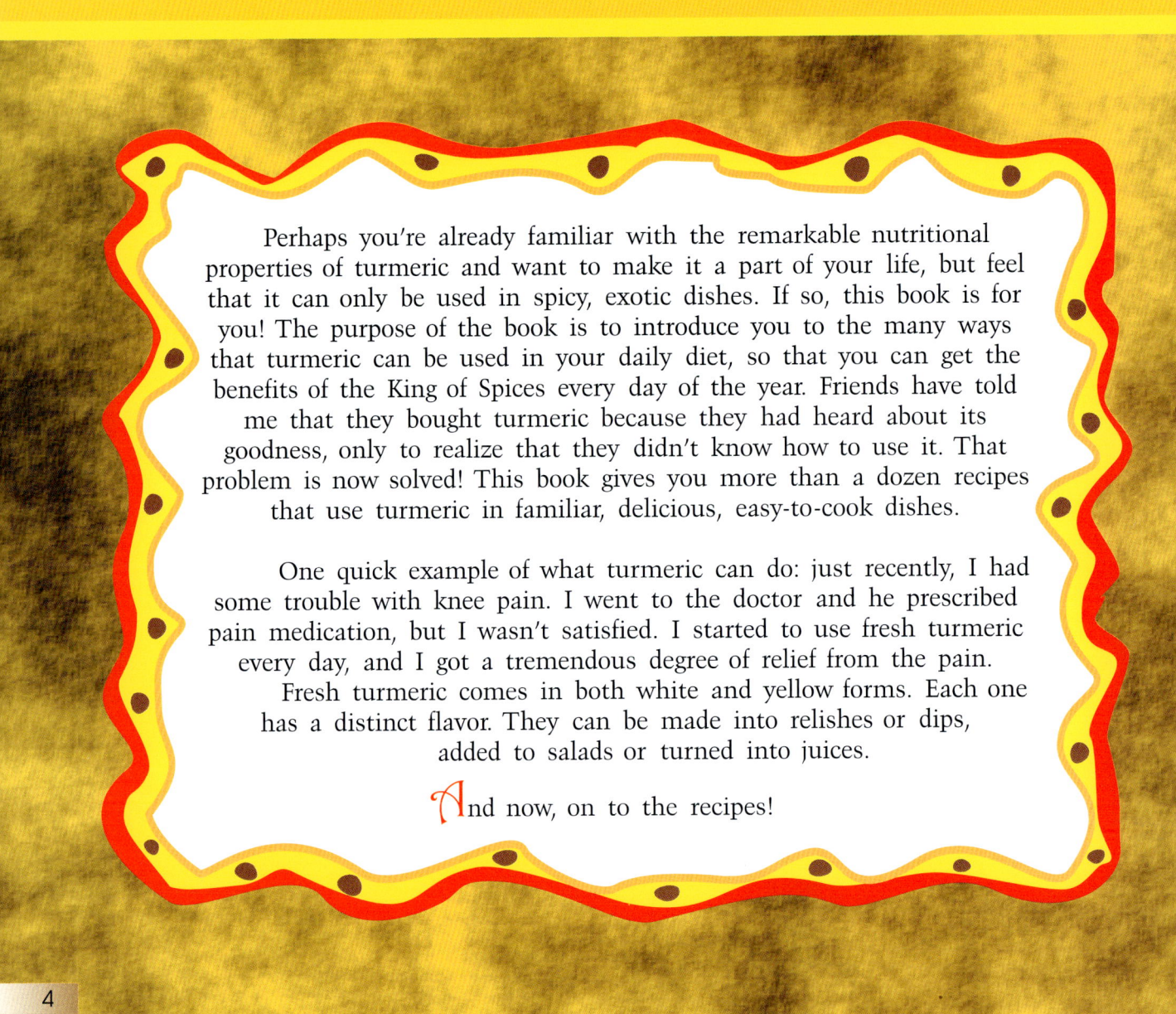

Perhaps you're already familiar with the remarkable nutritional properties of turmeric and want to make it a part of your life, but feel that it can only be used in spicy, exotic dishes. If so, this book is for you! The purpose of the book is to introduce you to the many ways that turmeric can be used in your daily diet, so that you can get the benefits of the King of Spices every day of the year. Friends have told me that they bought turmeric because they had heard about its goodness, only to realize that they didn't know how to use it. That problem is now solved! This book gives you more than a dozen recipes that use turmeric in familiar, delicious, easy-to-cook dishes.

One quick example of what turmeric can do: just recently, I had some trouble with knee pain. I went to the doctor and he prescribed pain medication, but I wasn't satisfied. I started to use fresh turmeric every day, and I got a tremendous degree of relief from the pain. Fresh turmeric comes in both white and yellow forms. Each one has a distinct flavor. They can be made into relishes or dips, added to salads or turned into juices.

And now, on to the recipes!

Introduction

These days we hear so many wonderful-sounding health claims about so many different herbs and spices that it's hard to know what to believe. But I can say from a lifetime of experience that turmeric is undoubtedly the most useful and versatile natural ingredient on earth.

Even a partial list of what turmeric can do is nothing short of astounding. Thousands of years of practical use have established that turmeric can relieve pain (it has long been used against arthritis), reduce joint inflammation, ease stomach disorders, prevent tooth decay, relieve skin conditions, lower cholesterol levels and improve heart and liver function. It is also helpful in the treatment of various types of inflammatory bowel diseases.

White and yellow fresh turmeric pieces

A Touch of Turmeric

How to Use the
King of Spices
in Your Daily Diet

by
Evelyn Banker